Fugitive Dreams

Fugitive Dreams

Poems by
Sowŏl Kim

Selected & translated by
JAIHIUN KIM &
RONALD B. HATCH

RONSDALE PRESS
1998

FUGITIVE DREAMS: Poems by Sowŏl Kim
Copyright English translation © 1998 Jaihiun Kim

RONSDALE PRESS
3350 West 21st Avenue
Vancouver, B.C. Canada
V6S 1G7

Set in Garamond 11-1/2 on 15
Typesetting: Julie Cochrane, Vancouver, BC
Printing: Hignell Printing, Winnipeg, Manitoba
Cover Design: Julie Cochrane

Ronsdale Press wishes to thank the Canada Council for the Arts, the Department of Heritage, and the British Columbia Cultural Services Branch for their support of its publishing program.

CANADIAN CATALOGUING IN PUBLICATION DATA
Kim, So-wŏl, 1902–1934.
   Fugitive dreams

   Poems.
   ISBN 0-921870-56-6

   I. Kim, Jaihiun, 1934–   II. Hatch, Ronald B.   III. Title.
PL991.415.C5A25 1998   895.7'13   C98-910071-5

ACKNOWLEDGEMENTS

—

Ronsdale Press wishes to thank Ajou University
for its financial assistance to the publication
of *Fugitive Dreams*.

ABOUT THE TRANSLATORS

—

JAIHIUN KIM is Professor of English at Ajou University, Korea. Born and brought up in Korea, he received his education in both Korea and the U.S.A., where he studied English literature and creative writing at the University of Massachusetts. Internationally known and recognized as a major poet in Korea, Professor Kim has translated well over two thousand Korean poems into English and published over a dozen volumes of his own poems, written in both English and Korean. In addition, he has translated volumes of American, English, Caribbean and Canadian poets into Korean.

RONALD B. HATCH is the Director and Chief Literary Editor of Ronsdale Press and Professor of English at the University of British Columbia. He has written extensively on both British and Canadian literature, and has a particular interest in the poetry of Asia.

—

The translators had two major aims in their translation of Sowŏl's poetry into English. The first was to remain faithful to Sowŏl's meaning while retaining as much of the original tonality as possible. The second was to render the poems in an idiom that sounded natural to the contemporary ear. Yet every act of translation is an act of interpretation, and each choice of English word or phrase, syntax, idiom, rhythm or rhyme — which all follow English rules and habits, and not Korean — risks separating the translation from the original. This risk is even greater with Sowŏl Kim, a poet whose subtlety of expression is wedded to his musicality. Nevertheless, it is the translators' hope that they have captured Sowŏl's intentions in language that is readable as poetry in its own right.

CONTENTS

—

FOREWORD

—

Better known by his pen name Sowŏl Kim, or Sowŏl for short (the name means "Simple Moon"), Chŏngshik Kim was born in 1902 and brought up in a small town in the far north of North Korea. After high school, he studied for a time in Japan. Although he did not finish his formal studies, he was widely read in Western literature as well as the Chinese classics. While happy in his marriage, he never found it easy to make a living, and he often resorted to drinking to escape from unpleasant realities. In 1934, at age thirty-two, he died an early and tragic death.

Sowŏl's personal distress could not, however, hide his talents as a poet. As early as 1920, when he was a young boy of seventeen, his artistic genius appeared in a series of poems which included "Flowers in the Mountains" and "Spring Traveller," published in *Ch'angjo* (Creation), the most influential literary magazine of the time. Those were followed by another string of fine lyrics, including "The Azaleas" in 1922, which reads in part:

> If you go away
> sick of the sight of me
> I'll let you go without a word.

> But I'll also gather by the armful
> the azaleas flaming on Yaksan, Yongbyon
> and scatter them in your path.

> Tread gently
> and lightly
> as you pass.

Simple in structure and economic in wording, "The Azaleas" is exquisitely musical and emotive, illustrating Sowŏl's technique of linking blunt, colloquial phrases such as "sick of the sight of me" with light, lyrical lines, as when the departing beloved is cautioned to "Tread gently / and lightly / as you pass" over the azaleas the poet has spread in her path.

Almost all of his lyric masterpieces were written in a period of five years betwen 1920 and 1925. Shocked by his suicide, some readers have taken comfort in the belief that Sowŏl must have written himself out before his death. Whatever the case, no other poet in Korea has commanded a larger audience; no one is ever likely to rival his popularity.

Sowŏl's poetry has been described, in the words of Richard Rutt, as the ideal verse for young people because its simplicity, vulnerability and tenderness make it readily accessible. But it could equally well be described as poetry for the learned because of its fascinating amalgam of elements from Korean folksong and Sowŏl's own highly personal and native sensitivity to the use of Korean speech. He is unmistakably one of Korea's greatest and most admired poets.

Although the tradition of Korean poetry extends over many centuries, the movement styled "Modernism" in Korea began only in the 1920s when a handful of poets formed themselves into a group named *Paekcho* (White Tide). For the Western reader it may seem curious, but the Korean Modernist movement also included many Romantic tendencies, since Korean writers were introduced to Modernism and Romanticism at the same moment. Like their counterparts in Europe, the members of *Paekcho* tended to look inwards, seeking in their own lives the sensations that could represent external social conditions. The general tone that pervaded the group was sombre and melancholy, with a strong dash of the decadence of the symbolist movement. Although Sowŏl was not directly connected to the "White Tide" group, his poetry derives from the same impulse, although possessing various different characteristics, perhaps the most significant being the way in which he was the first to employ plain language as a vehicle of communication. He also developed a deeply conscious interest in nature, not only as a source of beauty but also as a means of providing intimations about life and truth. He saw beauty in the fallen leaves, in the flush of sunset and lost love. A bird on the wing, or a fleecy tissue of cloud revealed to him the essentials of the human condition: the evanescence and vanity implicit in existence.

One of the most important influences on Sowŏl was his high school teacher and mentor, Anso Kim (1896–19??), who introduced the early Yeats of the Innisfree period to Sowŏl. Yet if one is thinking of Sowŏl's use of the ordinary language of everyday people, then perhaps an equally important influence is the work of Robert Burns, for Sowŏl developed his poetry from the vernacular sentiments of people living in the countryside, a countryside that he saw as unstained by the urban, commercial values of the city. What Sowŏl has to say in his "The Theory of Poetry" throws some light on his understanding of poetry:

> While the city boasts of din, splendour and the power of civilization, a solitary insect chirring in the grass or at the edge of the woods expresses more fully the essence of humanity — the sense of longing. A reed swaying in the storm laments the mutability and transiency of existence. Even as the insect and the reed are our companions and mentors, the leaping waves on the blue of the ocean demonstrate the human love of freedom.

Through his poetry, Sowŏl has exerted a decisive influence on modern Korean verse and has established a major tradition among contemporary writers. Despite the seeming negativism to which he could at times succumb, he developed in his poems the grace inherent in resignation, a grace which transcends despair and glories in things lost or about to vanish — the triumph of his art.

— Jaihiun Kim

The Azaleas

—

If you go away,
sick of the sight of me,
I'll let you go without a word.

But I'll also gather by the armful
the azaleas flaming in Yaksan, Yongbyon
and scatter them in your path.

Tread gently
and lightly
as you pass.

If you go away,
sick of the sight of me,
I will weep no tears, though I die without you.

The azaleas, a genus of rhododendrons with funnel-shaped pink corollas, bloom
profusely on the hills and mountainsides across the country in the springime. The aza-
lea has been designated as the national flower of North Korea since the country was
divided into two political entities, North and South Korea, after the Second World
War.

Yaksan is a scenic site noted for azaleas in the country of Yongbyon, North Pyong-an
Province in North Korea.

Flowers in the Mountains

—

Flowers bloom
in the mountains;
spring, summer and all through autumn
flowers bloom.

In the mountains
far-off and near
flowers bloom,
beyond and apart in solitude.

Little birds trill
in the mountains;
for the love of flowers
they live in the mountains.

Flowers fade
in the mountains;
spring, summer and all through autumn
flowers fade.

Korea is a mountainous country, approximately two-thirds of the land being covered by mountains. They range from hills and hillocks, 100 to 200 meters high in and near towns and villages, to high land masses and mountain ranges over 1,000 to 2,000 meters above sea level.

Love Song

—

My love's sweet melodies
haunt me, soothing my heart.

I listen to them all day
as I lean against the gate
till dusk descends,
and I sleep at nightfall.

My love's song in gentle ripples
rocks me to honeyed sleep.
Lying alone in bed,
sweet and sound I sleep.

But the moment I awake
my love's melodies are lost to me —
no sooner heard
than forgotten.

Lost Love

—

Unable to forget you may miss me,
you will carry me in memory
until the day you suddenly forget.

Unable to forget you may miss me,
you will remember me through the passing years
until the image falls away.

Then you may protest:
how could I ever forget
when tender passion tears me apart?

I Did Not Know Before

—

I did not know before
that the moon rises every night.

I did not know before
that I would miss you so much.

I did not know before
how to watch the brightest moon.

I did not know before
that the moon would be my sorrow.

Some Day

—

If you should call me some day
I would say: *"I've forgotten about you."*

If you should reproach me —
"I missed you much and had to give up."

If you should reproach me again —
"I've forgotten because I cannot trust you anymore."

Day after day I've been thinking of you
until some day I will say: *"I've forgotten."*

I Miss You

Before the spring is gone,
before flowers fade and scatter,
I wait for my beloved
to arrive before the setting of the sun.

The wind charges wildly
through the silvering mist.
The moon slants in the skies,
ending its nightly vigil.

My heart frets, ill at ease.
When can I see my beloved again?
Could we but delight together
in the serenade of birds!

Attachment

—

What keeps you from coming?
The window dapples in the shadow
of plum blossoms stirring under the moon.
I would rather sleep, eyes tightly shut.

Sound of the far distance.
Sound of the springtide.
Sound from the exquisite habitat, the Watery Kingdom.
Sound of nymphs chanting and dancing.
Sound of the springtide.

In my heart, dark and deep,
in the bright mirror where a spring cloud drifts,
the haloed moon beams and the gentle rain drips.
What keeps you from coming?

Awake or Asleep

—

Awake or asleep, up or down,
I once had a friend following me, shadow-like.

How we've frittered away the years
caught in futile cares.

Again today in tears I leave you,
your heart churning.

Hurt and forsaken, my heart aches
and I know it's all for love.

To My Beloved

—

I would sit up in your thoughts
many a sleepless night.
And still I often think of you
as dreams circle my tear-soaked pillow.

At the crossroads in a strange land
I turn twenty, sadness my mantle in the falling dusk.
I roam in the plains in the gloom of night
and you are a forgotten sorrow.

When I think of you
tears drop like rain into sand.
As dreams circle my tear-soaked pillow
you are a forgotten sorrow.

Invocation

O, name shattered.
O, name vanished into thin air.
O, name without response to my call.
O, name I will be calling till death.

You've gone before, I have said,
one last word etched on my heart.
O, my love nearest my heart,
nearest my heart.

The red sun hangs over the western peaks.
Even a herd of deer laments.
I am calling to you
as I stand on a lone hill.

I call to you till sorrow chokes me,
sorrow chokes me.
But my voice rings hollow in the vast void
between heaven and earth.

Should I turn to stone
I will be calling to you.
O, my love nearest my heart,
nearest my heart.

Love Pillow

—

Shall I gnash my teeth
and drop dead?
The moon sheds its dappled beams
on the window.

In tears, I lie curled up,
resting my head on my arm.
A spring pheasant screams,
sleepless, in the night.

Where has the love pillow
gone now
that once we both shared, pledging
to each other an oath of lasting love?

On the spring hillside
a cuckoo keeps carolling
calling its mate.

Where has the love pillow
gone now?
The moon sheds its dappled beams
on the window.

The Lonesome Day

—

On the day
your letter arrived
a sad rumour started abroad.

When you said, *"Throw it into the stream,"*
I took it to mean that I should remember
you even in dreams.

Almost illegible,
in plain vernacular script,
you wrote down tears.

"Throw it into the stream"
must have meant tears were blinding your eyes,
and that I should read with tenderness.

Grass Plucking

—

The grass grows green on the hillsides.
The brook threads through the bushes
and shadows drift over the sandy bed.

Where is my beloved to be found?
My thought of her blooms every day
as I sit alone on the hill
and pluck grass to toss on the waters.

As they drift down the brook
the blades of grass spread in a thin sheet,
the waves rippling in my heart.

Where is my beloved to be found?
Nowhere to put my mind at ease,
I pluck grass to toss on the waters
and my heart warms to the floating grass.

What My Love Said

—

You've been gone these two months,
scum filming the water in the jar.
Your invitation to come with you
strikes me as a curse.

The grass flames green in spring.
Like a tree, its roots struck off,
or a bird wounded in its wings,
I'll have no more flowering days in store.

Every night before cockcrow
I'll go out to greet your return.
When a sliced moon slants over the hill crest
I'll bid you farewell, blessed spirit.

Years run like a river.
Your invitation to come with you
must be a reminder that I should give up;
I cannot forget till death, though.

Parting

—

With these words spoken:
"I'll miss you,"
I miss you even more.

Shall I just leave?
Yet one more wish
and this time for the last time.

The crows caw in chorus
in the hills and fields
as if to announce sundown.

The currents of the stream
course unendingly along
urging each other
to pull and push.

A Purple Cloud

—

A purple cloud drifts away
and the sky begins to clear.
The snow fallen stealthily in the night
bursts the pine grove into blossom.

Millions of flashing flakes
dazzle in the sunlight.

I gaze on them forgetful
of what happened during the night.

A purple cloud drifts away.

A Desire to Meet

—

The country road darkens after sunset.
Murky clouds over the far-off peaks merge in darkness.
I can hardly resist this urge to meet my beloved.
She will not come, I know. Who will come tonight
that blind steps lead me on?
At moonrise a wild goose screams across the sky.

After Being Ruined

—

Waking from a sad dream
I rush
into the fields

where rain drizzles,
and frogs' voices tear the air
in the gloom of the grass.

Loitering, eyes downcast, hands folded behind,
I hear someone intone
in the glowworm-filled bushes: Farewell, be prosperous.

Dreaming of Old Days

—

Snow is falling, falling outside.
The moonlight steals through the window.
Dusk-borne, she enters my dream
to be held in my arms.

Tears soak my pillow
now she has left me.
At quiet dawn a shadowy star
peeps through the window.

Tears Stream Down

—

Tears stream down my cheeks
when a yearning for you grips me.
Tears stream down without end.

You're forever imprinted on my mind;
I've never broken with you.
Yet tears stream down my cheeks.

My heart loaded with grief,
tears stream down my face
when I think of you —
perhaps because we parted against our fate.

Dream-Reunion

—

Far into the night
faint lights glimmer red.

A footfall, faint,
barely audible,
dies away.

Unable to sleep alone,
I turn and twist all night.

Far into the night
faint lights glimmer red.

Untitled

—

I miss the place where my beloved is.
I miss her because I cannot serve her.
Don't you ever watch the birds winging
north and south, drawn home by instinct?

In Autumn Morning

—

Under the far-off, pale-blue sky
rows of grey roofs flash.
The wind whines in the wood
through the ribbed trees.
Mists invade a mountain village
barely visible in the distance.

The rain has chilled the dawn air.
The stream freezes, studded with fallen leaves.
Memories coming alive in tears
whisper comfortingly to my soul
that cries wildly like an infant
cut with a knife.

Wasn't there a time
when you were happy and light-hearted?
How the voice soothes,
a salve to my bruised heart.
I cry and cry at the voice,
without shame or hate.

In Autumn Evening

—

The waters gleam white, stretching farther than the sky.
And the clouds are tinted redder than the sun.
Sad, on the edge of the uprolling plains
I wander tearfully, alive with grief.

My steps lure me into the thickening shade.
The road stretches endlessly ahead.
A riverside village looms
through the bare branches of trees.

No one is expected.
Who should I wait for?
I would rather pace the pondside
with the flush of sunset glowing in the waters.

Hands Joined in Prayer

—

We stroll out, and night lights suffuse us.
Look, come under the leafy branches,
we can converse while walking in the breeze.

Streets come alive in the lamplight. In the dim vault
of the sky, a shadow-like star sparkles far away
as dew glistens in the grass.

Night has fallen and stillness holds all.
Our footsteps slow, as if spell-bound.
Stopping short we face each other, eyes shut.
From a distant mountain temple a bell booms,
the moon holding a wake.

Spring Hill

The green meadow, velvet-soft,
is ready to shout in glee.
The bright sunbeams glance
tenderly to the eye.

In purpling violets
and golden daisies,
bees and butterflies drug themselves
to honeyed sleep.

Peach and apricot trees
flush as if drunk with wine.
And the leafing willows dance away,
their locks let loose.

Driven by a new master, the ox
lows sadly homeward.
The dog stretches blissfully
after a carefree nap.

In the lush of green grass,
in the flaming cataracts of flowers,
my love and I once made merry
with our arms locked in dream.

Before Sundown

—

Some time before sundown
the air thins and hollows.
Treetops moan in winds that sweep
the lavender sky with wheeling pigeons.

Some time before sundown
the air frets with restlessness.
Why can't we ease into joy?
A way-worn wanderer may as well turn in.

Crows flail by in a flock,
a bell resonates faintly from afar,
a calf lows softly,
a dog bays at the skies.

Some time before sundown
untold sadness pervades the air.
Shall I head for the shade of a spreading zelkova
by the river and cry my heart out in private?

Some time before sundown
Loving-kindness suffuses us.
Why don't you come to me?
Shall we wear a monk's robe and pray to Buddha?

Some time before sundown
tenderness overflows.
Why don't we walk out onto the reach of sand
and wait for the moon to joyfully greet us?

Mother and Sisters

Mother and sisters, we'll live together by the river
with a sandbar blooming golden for our garden
and reeds fluting music from behind the gate.
Mother and sisters, we'll live together by the river.

Untitled

—

Mummy, the sun has risen again today.
Mother dead is so lovely
while mother alive is so wicked.
Mummy, this is how I go on without you.
Today, as ever, I miss you.

Green Meadow

—

Green,
green meadow
flaming golden.
The fire in the remote mountains spreads
over the grass on my loved one's grave.
Spring has arrived with her vernal colours.
Spring has brought her splendour
to grace the willow tips,
the green meadow, the remote mountains and rivers.

Song by the Brook

—

Were you a wind
you might brush my lapels in the bleak plains
where a brook runs, moonbeamed.

Were you born a slug
we might dream idly together
on a murky mountain pass in the rainy night.

Were you born a stone
on the cliffs by the shore
I would hug you and roll into the sea below.

Were I a flaming spirit
I would burn your heart all night
till both of us turn to ashes.

Life and Death

—

"Alive is as good as dead."
It sounds sensible enough to say,
for a man lives till death comes with age.
Why should I weep today on a mountaintop
as if I were alone in misery?

The Sea Goes Dry

—

This grief of mine defies control.
Flowers cascade down, their petals
drifting in the late spring evening.
As an old saying goes:
"the sea dries into a mulberry field."
What youth once gloried in
— a vision of beauty — turns sour
and falls away into forgetfulness.
Look! Aren't you sad to see
those flowers bleeding red
cataracts at the close of a spring day
in the month of March?

The Sea

—

Where is the sea that grows pink weeds
as the playful waves rise and sink?

Where is the sea on which fishermen
sing of love?

Where is the sea that takes its hue
from the sky turning purple at sunset?

Where is the sea over which way-worn
birds wander in flocks?

Where is the sea that beckons
to the strange land somewhere beyond?

The Scops Owl

—

Choptong!
Choptong! —
Listen, my brothers:

the sister-spirit returns
to complain at her old home
by the riverside.

Ages ago there lived by the river
in the remote part of the country
a girl who took her own life
because of her stepmother's envy.

Shall I call her my sister,
a pitiful soul?
Driven by jealousy she died,
transformed into a scops owl.

Missing her nine brothers,
left behind, she returns to complain
sadly in the dead of night
flying over mountain after mountain.

The scops owl is often mistaken for the nightingale or cuckoo.

Spring Rain

—

Caught in a sudden shower, spring sobs,
while flowers fall everywhere —
even in my heart.
Watch, as the clouds drift high over the budding branches
until dusk descends with nightfall.
The sweet, sad rain falls endlessly
as do my tears on the carpet of flowers.

Wind and Spring

—

The spring wind and the windy spring.
The spring wind sways the trees
as it stirs my heart in the windy spring.
With spring and its wind
I weep over wine and flowers.

Innocence

—

"*Once gone, never to return*" —
I heard it said when young and green.
If only I could see my beloved again
to whom I bade farewell as I left the graveyard.

So young I didn't know a thing.
Now with lips redolent of the sweet and bitter
I know how to conjure with the world.
Would that I could live over
my youthful, innocent days.

"*Once gone, out of mind*" —
How could I make out its drift?
May the flame in the remote mountains
consume the grass on my beloved's grave.

Old Familiar Faces

—

Thinking ends in slumber;
forgetting fetches longing.
Don't talk, my love — from now on
sorrow will be a stranger to our old familiar faces.

The Grave

—

A voice is calling to me, calling.
The rows of gravestones dotting
the reddish mounds sway in the moonlight.
My tuneless song modulates to sorrow
as I search for ancestral annals
long interred.
My song spreads, traceless, over the mounds
that lie dimmed in shadows.
A voice is calling to me,
calling to me, calling,
as if invoking my soul.

The Lonely Grave

—

On this grave dug in my heart since we parted
spring brings no flowers.

You have been gone these ten years
and each spring renews my thought of you.

All fades and is forgotten, so they say,
yet the old days remain sad and unforgotten.

With nowhere to ease my restless mind
I turn sadly inwards to greet the spring.

Remarriage

—

After the death of her husband
she will remarry, it's been rumoured.
What can be wrong with that when she has led
a lonely life these ten years?
This is the way of the world.

Until the turn of the century, a woman's remarriage was regarded as a social taboo.

Man and Wife

—

My dear wife, my sweet love,
isn't it heaven's will for us to live
in mutual trust?
Is there any need to argue?
Strange and inscrutable is mankind.
Can't you say it's true? or false?
Our two minds bound in love
can spurn discord.
Two score and ten, or a little less,
is our marriage span.
What is the lasting tie of love?
Let me make my will that after death
we shall be interred in one place.

Memory

—

Hugging in my heart a dream,
hazy and traceless,
I lean like a child on the gate
and gaze at the sky where clouds pass.

I stand on tiptoe to reach the sky-rim
only to find no path for my dreams.
Clouds scud back and forth across the blue
that stays forever constant.

Like a root stirring with life,
like a faithful heart that never fails,
dreams will bloom in the thorny path of memory
as the green grass sprouts in the stony fields.

Cockcrow

—

In your absence
cockcrow scares me.

When day dawns
and sleep escapes me,
dreams flee.

Hurt and bruised,
I weary of life,

wandering lonely in the grass,
dappled in the dawn of shadows.

Parents

—

When leaves fall rustling
into the long winter night
I sit face to face with my mother
and listen to an old tale.

How is it that I was born
to be her listener?
Don't ask me, I will find out
when I am finally a parent.

Wax Candles

—

Wax candles burn low and gutter,
flickering against the blueish window.
Sleepless in the stillness of night
I lose myself in the mirror.
Looking absent-spirited at myself
I think aloud: mankind passes the first
few nights in dream, then death
approaches when he is napping
and the candle is suddenly snuffed.

Though the Sun Sets

—

The flush of sunset fades
over the mountains because of you.

The sunrise glowing over the mountains
must be your morning grandeur.

Should the earth sink and heaven cave in,
you are the only excuse for my being.

Drawn to you only in thought now,
I'll soon be with you like a shadow.

O my love, how you burnt my heart once!

Sealed-up Pledge

—

When I wake in bed from a bad dream,
when the grass sprouts in the springtime,
when a fair youth passes me by,
I suddenly call to mind our almost
forgotten pledge, sealed like fate.

Solemnity

—

Alone I climb a hilltop,
while in the pouring morning sun
the grass blades glisten
and the wind whispers.
Yet
battered and bruised,
my heart aches
and again I sense in all humanity
the solemnity of living.

Dawn

On the pondside ankle-deep in fallen leaves
trees cast their jagged shadows
while waters awaken a pale sheen.
I stand alone waiting
for the day to dawn.
Are there tender tears heavenly people shed,
like a rain-cloud, on their lonely dream pillows?
My sweet, why don't you come, shy and soft,
over to me across the waters?
A cloud braces against the evening skies.
A half moon holds a wake in mid-heaven.

Road

—

Again last night
in a country inn
I heard a crow cawing all night.

Today
where shall I be bound?
How many more miles to go?

Up to the mountains,
onto the plains?
No, no place beckons.

No more talk.
To my home in the far north
trains and boats travel.

Tell me,
wild goose in the skies,
is there a sky-road that you travel so freely?

Wild goose in the skies,
look at me standing
at the crossroads.

The road radiates
in many directions
yet none of them can I choose.

Spring Traveller

—

Across the steep mountains
fording the curving rivers
how sadly I must wander
in the fair flowers and green grass.

Maple trees leafing yellow,
early willows budding fast,
as the wind blows hard
and the sun sinks early.

A lone inn by the mountain lane
stands bleak and lonesome.
A way-worn peddler has turned in
and complains of his trade in sleep-talk.

Shadows close in after sunset
how much farther still to go?
A simple place will do
for the night on the road.

Mist silvers over the woods
and birds grow frightened of the moon.
I tenderly think of you
in the sweet spring night.

Silken Mist

—

When silken mist spreads over the snowy fields,
we are lost in fond remembrance.
Madly missing each other
we weep at reunion.

When silken mist spreads over the snowy fields,
solitary souls can hardly stand their lonely lives.
As the snow melts on tree branches, young girls run about,
their sashes streaming from their necks.

When silken mist spreads over the snowy fields,
skylarks soar in the skies
and we become drunk with things on earth —
the sky, the sea and the fields.

When silken mist spreads over the snowy fields,
we are lost in fond remembrance:
how we fell in love for the first time
and were forever parted.

My Friend's Abode

When fleecy petals drift
in the village edged with willows
we once cried in the snow under the moon
holding each other lest we be torn apart.

Giving my word to meet in three years
I set out on the dark waves of the sea
and said goodbye to the red pennants
fluttering along the pierside.

Night's far gone in this room at the inn,
the wick of youth is burning low.
When I learned of his death
grief gripped like a vise.

I saw the last of him carried across the hills
ridge after ridge, only to be buried
in a handful of earth
lashed by the rain.

My year-long wish for reunion
ended with a mouldering
mound, a rude heap
in a small neglected corner.

Even now lying quietly in bed,
Washed in cold sweat, I hear papered windows
whistling, and his shadow hovers as in the days
when we would rollick together on a reed-horse.

The Sky's Edge

—

Irresistibly,
I rush out of my home onto the mountain top
and look out over the ocean
where a ship sails to the sky's edge.

Cloud

—

If I could make a stallion
of the crimson cloud that sails
darkened in the night,
I would fly nine thousand leagues
to be held in your arms
while you lie asleep.
But this I cannot do.
When you hear the rain fall,
take it for my tears
that I shed every night.

Uneasy Feeling

—

The day you were expected
you did not come.
I felt quite wrongly
that you would come.
The sun has already set
dusk gathers.

Snowy Evening

—

In the windless evening
when snow falls thick and fast
what are you doing
this time of the year?

What if I should dream?
Meet my beloved in my sleep?
Long forgotten my love will come with the snow.
Toward evening snow falls thick and fast.

My Home

—

In this place
far from the world of men,
I decide to stay for the night.

In the distant sky
a boat sails away,
trailing a departure melody.

From my closed eyes
tears
run down my face.

In dreams or awake I see my home clearly.
The clouds pass continously
over the mountains one behind another.

My House

—

I will build myself a house
at the foot of a detached hill
far from the seashore.
Then I will open a road in front
so that people can go by,
alone, without companions.
With the sun sunk in the pale shallows,
I will stand at my gate, expectant.
Birds call in the dawning shades,
the world glistens calm and white.
And from the bright morning hours
I will watch every passer-by
on the chance of meeting my beloved.

Paper Kite

The sun slants on an afternoon crossroads
the early winter darkens in the streets.
Leaning blankly on the door frame
I watch a paper kite flash like a snowflake.

Red Tides

—

When those red tides driven by the wind
begin to roll shoreward
I wish to ride, ensconced in a purple cloud,
on the wings of the wind, embracing
the fiery ball of the sun, and leaping high
as the red tides surge shoreward.

Picnicking

—

Flowers in the fields
bloom and soon
scatter.

The grass in the fields
grows thick and tall.
A last year's snakeskin
streams in the shifting winds.

Look, all things around
brighten as the pulse quickens.
A kite soars in the skies,
its wings widespread.

At this time of year
I take to the open road,
my heart exulting
as my steps carry me onwards.

The First-Worn Skirt

—

Spring departs, the day is done
flowers fade at the close of spring.
I cry futilely over the fading flowers
and feel empty over the departing spring.
Pulled apart from home, holding
a mossy, leafless branch,
I cry wildly at the setting of the sun
and hardly notice that my new skirt
is stained with tears.
I cry futilely over the fading flowers
and feel empty over the departing spring.

Sowŏl here speaks in the voice of a young woman.

Dream Visitor

—

As I grow older
a secret visitor calls on me
and wakes me into dream.
Foxy-hued, slim-fingered,
in a mysterious yet familiar motion
she comes and nestles in my arms.
A word begins to form,
but then she stops
and silence envelops us.
Soon she starts up at a cock's wingbeat:
alert in the broad daylight
I take every passer-by for someone else.

Night

—

This loneliness teases me out of sleep.
I miss you so much my whole body aches.
Parted for so long
I fear lest I recognize you.

Darkness has settled
in this famed port-town of Chemulpo
where night passes in a drizzling rain
and the salt wind chills me through.

Lying quietly, so quietly,
I hear, my vision blurred,
the frothing springtide sob
As it surges shoreward.

Chemulpo is the old name for Inch'on, a port city west of Seoul.

At Evening

—

Plowmen have driven their oxen home
leaving the fields to frogs whose voices rend the air.
The skies descend lower, the mountain pass darkens.
Birds return to tall treetops for the night.

I gaze on the gleaming waters
that wind through the wilderness.
Immobile, my head hanging low,
I heave a sigh, I know not why.

Have I really come so far tonight?
I'm floating feather-light,
and as my spirit soars,
suddenly through the reeds, the glint of stars.

Two People

—

Flake after flake
fleecy snow falls
carpeting the mountain pass.
Straw-sandaled, with leggings fastened,
a knap-sack on my back,
I start on my way, then turn around
to catch sight of her form, almost
erased.

The Great Wall

—

Night after night
all night long
the Great Wall is built
and pulled down.

Mountain

—

Even a mountain bird cries
in an alder tree; it longs
for home beyond the ridge
of mountains.

Snow piles up as it falls.
Seventy or so leagues
yet to go today.
Once I turned back after sixty leagues.

No return. No, never to return.
I shall not return to Samsu-kapsan.
Though I should try not to remember
fifteen years of attachment cannot be forgotten.

Snow falls in the mountains and melts in the fields.
Even a mountain bird cries
in an alder tree.
Steep is the pass leading to Samsu-Kapsan.

Samsu-kapsan is a place in North Korea, suggestive of a dungeon.

Samsu-kapsan

dedicated to my mentor Anso Kim

Why did I come to Samsu-kapsan. Where can it be?
A place of impending cliffs, a world of peaks and rapids.

Would that I could go back home, but I cannot return.
Samsu-kapsan lies at the world's edge, its path rough and steep.

Where can Samsu-kapsan be? Once in, never out.
I shall never see my old home. If only I were a bird . . .

I cannot return to my beloved, I cannot.
Cruel is my fate. Would that I could go back home,

but Samsu-kapsan locks me up.
No way out of its clutches. No return but to despair.

By the Brook

—

What has brought you
to sit alone brooding
by the brook?

When the green grass flames
and the wavelets dimple
in the spring breeze,

you may have given your word
that you will be gone —
but not for good.

Why then do you brood
as you sit by the brook
day after day?

Because of your promise
that you will be gone, but not for good —
and wish to be remembered.

Sakchu-kusong

—

Three days by boat and waterborne,
three thousand li away.
Again three thousand li on foot: this place
is six thousand li beyond the mountains.

Even swallows turn back halfway,
rain-drenched, caught in the storms.
The mountains shoot up at evening
and tower in the night.

Sakchu-kusong is far away.
Six thousand li beyond the mountains.
Often in dreams I go four or five thousand li
only to turn back again.

The farther apart, the more the attachment.
I miss the place where my beloved is.
Don't you see how these birds long for home
as they wing north and south through the sky.

Where would those clouds stay overnight
scudding over the edge of the far fields?
Sakchu-kusong is far away,
six thousand li beyond the mountains.

Sakchu-kusong is the name of twin towns in North Korea.
One li equals 0.4 km.

On the Mountain Top

—

On the mountain top that overlooks
the expanse of the impassable ocean
I see my beloved's home
float before me as in a dream sky.

Onto the sand-stretched pierside,
a boatman's idyllic songs waft in from the sea.
Mist thickens toward twilight
and waves break into spray in the distance.

Night falls and waterbirds moan.
Boats head one after another
for the deep sea till they drift
like tiny leaves far into the distance.

I pass the night in the mountains.
Washed in the flush of the morning sun,
I listen to the water rippling
beneath my loved one's window.

Should she ever call to me,
awakened by my water song,
I would lie fast asleep in the mountains:
nobody knows my whereabouts.

Wangshimni

—

It is raining
incessantly.
Fall, rain —
hopefully for days on end.

The 8th and 20th of the month
will bring rain, and it may stop
on the 1st and 15th, it is said.
Rain is falling on the endless road to Wangshimni.

Hear me, bird.
Cry if you want to
far beyond Wangshimni.
A field bird calls, limp and rain-soaked.

The slender willows loosen their hair
in Ch'onan where three roads converge.
Fall, rain — hopefully for days on end.
Even the clouds moan, moored on the mountain ridge.

Wangshimni was formerly a suburban area of Seoul.

Ch'onan is a city south of Seoul noted for its willows.

Sweetheart and Friend

—

A friend gladdens us when we are sad,
love sweetens us while we are in love.
When flowering strawberries scent the air,
when peppers ripen red in the night,
you sing and I will drink.

Face to Face with a Lamp

—

When I sit lonely
face to face with a burning lamp
I wish to cry my heart out.
Who can tell why?

When I lie lonely in the dark night
I wish to cry with abandon.
Who can tell why?
I could blame others, but would it help?

A Half Moon

—

For how long has it been up,
suspended pale in the skies?
The wind rises; nightfall brings a chill.
The sun has sunk in the gleaming waters.

Cold mist hovers over the fields
dark and devoid of grass.
In the dead of winter
grief weighs me down.

Love has gone, dampening my heart's flame.
Youth will soon turn to age.
Bramble vines darken in the fields
dropping their dead in the faint evening light.

Changbyoli

—

The beauty spot in Pyongyang,
Changbyoli blazes in a lavender meadow.
The rain falls aslant
in silver and golden threads.

On the coarse snake-patterned shade
the mist descends
in fine, thin filaments.

Waterbirds wheel in a flock
over the middle reaches of Taedong River.
When we were about to part
rain fell endlessly.

Changbyoli is a scenic place on the outskirts of Pyongyang, which is now the capital of
North Korea.

Taedong River flows through Pyongyang, North Korea.

Chance

—

A bridge used to span this river.
The raging waters of time
washed it away while I stood
hesitating.

What a fool I was not to cross it
in response to your call.
Now we see each other
only at a distance, eyes filled with tears.

Thousands of Miles

—

A wild urge
prompts me to speed
thousands of miles.
Were I to follow this path,
arrow-straight to the end,
I might see strands of smoke
rising from mountains on fire.

Riverside Village

—

At moonrise after nightfall
the river laps gleaming white
and sand spangles golden
as a bride-groom passes on muleback.

Here nestles a riverside village
where I live alone
passing sadly the late spring days
seized by a craving
for blessed marriage —
an old bachelor,
I live alone in the riverside village.

Meditation

—

In the quiet and chill of the night,
perched on the windowsill, legs dangling,
I hear frogs serenading.
What a pity you've retired alone!

In my pensive mood I see lights glimmering
through the bush, the village exorcising demons.
The incantation dies away in the end,
the chorus of frogs is stilled, my mind is calm
and peace spreads outwards from heaven to earth.

I rise and proceed to share your bed.
All is immobile; stillness holds all.
Stars twinkling on high
draw me closer and closer.

An Old Tale

—

When night falls, dark and quiet,
with a lamp burning low
I weep all alone endless tears
in pain and loneliness.
I used to pass my days without tears
in my small world
and rejoice in reciting an old tale
blind to any sorrow in store.

Since my beloved has gone
leaving me for good
all I have valued on earth
has gone one by one.

Yet the old tale I used to tell
remains with me, haunting me,
its plot thickening day by day.
It makes me cry to no purpose.

Home-Thought

—

I climb a mountaintop
and look out to the ocean;
a ferryboat floats on the blue
stretching a hundred miles around.

Where is the famous mountain, its famed temple?
The incense burner, its table and bamboo wares?
After the flush of setting sun fades behind the peaks
the waves of the sea stretch out for a hundred miles.

"When you return, fair youth,
come with glory and success."
The ferryboat is now far off:
how can I cross the wide ocean?

Pheasants breed in the mountains.
Pulled far apart from home,
I gaze on the mountains, heavy-hearted,
my vision blurred in tears.

How You Weep!

—

How you weep in misfortune!
I know what caused you to suffer
and harden your heart
blown about in the winds
driven by the tides
because of me.
Time and again
the red-rusty foam sprays
against the jagged boulders on the shore.
Dark-blue moss gathered in your heart.

I Long for My Love

—

On your soul
lovely and pure
rather than on your lips
red and tender
I press my burning lips.
And the forceful rhythm of my life
pulsates unendingly
in your heart.

Night Rain

—

Where shall I go, a hard-fated soul
wandering like running waters?

Shall I sidestep the steep mountains
or leap over the craggy rocks on the way?

Yet no way out is in view
sorrow loads my heart.

Perhaps my beloved is the night rain
roaming endlessly — just as I do.

Snow

—

The falling snow is trodden down.
Like ashes, it drifts and vanishes
wind-driven or melting in fire —
the heart of a woman, my own beloved.

Cricket

—

The wind sweeps through the mountains,
as the chill rain falls.
The night you tell of life's joys and sorrows
the fire in a charcoal-burner's hut dies out.
A cricket chirps.

An Ant

—

When azaleas bloom
and the wind sighs in the willows,
an ant, slender
in its waist,
becomes a busy architect, work-mad,
on a spring day.

Swallow

—

In the first flush of dawn
the swallow twittered
sadly as it winged to the south.

The swallow flew home,
the fresh of the morning
breeze its godspeed.

Weaned from the parent bird
and left behind, the swallow gazes
at the home skies.

A born wanderer,
it took off on the wing
in the fresh of the morning breeze.

Homesickness

—

How I yearn for the sea today
as the salt tears gather.
A memory of your tenderness,
the powder-soft touch of your hand,
and I tremble like an aspen,
a needle in my heart —
even as the sun blazes on the sea at home.

The Sky

—

The sky spreads higher and more blue
every day I gaze on it,
the blue turning always
to a sigh.

Foreign Country

—

I turn to look at an iron bridge
I've crossed before I realize
I've set foot in a foreign land.

Forgotten Mind

—

How lonely I have wandered
torn apart from home!
How is it that you're back
when flowers flare in the spring wind?
Lost to each other, we've become strangers.
Why should my old dreams visit me? —
returning in waves of grief.

Moonlight

The moon shines bright as crickets chirr
and I remember you and the night
when I held you tight like a fool.
Shall I take you along to Seoul tonight?

Dream

—

Even dogs and fowls
have dreams to dream — so some believe.
True, springtime is good for dreaming,
yet I go dreamless.
If only I could dream
and dream till I end my days . . .

Deep Faith Fails

—

As deep faith fails in the desert of my heart
I say to an old friend or two I meet on the way:
"You are no longer of help."

A Lump of Grief

—

With incense burning, I kneel in prayer,
a lump of grief stuck in my heart.
Under a sliced moon the rain moans as it falls,
a lump of grief stuck in my heart.

Love's Gift

These tears dripping for love,
these pearl-like tears,
I wish to string together
with an imperishable red thread
for my beloved to wear round her neck
as a gift of love.

Man Is Born to Live and Die

—

How many times a day do I ponder
on what I live for,
innocent of life, as it were?
How the river in the end
empties into the sea!
It seems senseless to complain
of strife and struggle; man is born
to live and die.
Yet I pause to contemplate,
like an ant lost in building its shelter
on a warm spring day.
I wish to live my life to the full
drunk with the joy of living.
If man is made by nature to live,
why should I strain, fret and fuss
for nothing?
Man is born to live and die.

An Owl

—

Last night
an owl came to hoot
at the back window of my room.
The overcast sky darkens the sea;
today ends without a glimpse of sun.

Fishermen

—

What bliss it is to be blind to life's futility.
Today as usual from the far-off village
a fishing boat has set out to sea, I hear —
how fearful were the waves billowing last year!

Delight

—

The sky sobs in its dark vault.
Slipping out of the maze of dreams,
an insomniac ghost glares, grief-laden.
The rain is lashing
the dark-shaded willows,
a mournful incantation.

Your daughter leaves home, wailing,
her raven hair let loose,
earthworms wriggle, a ghostly white,
the ebony sea spreads far and wide.
In the hollow of a dead tree
a woodpecker continues with his rat-a-tat-tat.

Optimism

—

I must take comfort,
take life as it comes
the way the wind whines in the trees
stripped of flowers and foliage.

Hope

—

Night comes and snow falls.
On the edge of a brook
I hear an owl hooting forever in the mountains.
Fallen leaves lie scattered under the snow.

What a bleak landscape —
a moment too late I realize
how to be wise after sorrow.
Things of this world
are an idle show,
the skin-deep beauty our mind creates.
In the sweet-scented autumn night
the trees throw twisting shadows
on leaves torn off by the lashing rain.

INDEX OF TITLES

—